C000080876

THE ORIGINAL

THE CAT

Artist Collection

THIS IS A CARLTON BOOK

The Cat Logos and Photographs © 2005
artlist INTERNATIONAL
Design copyright © 2005 Carlton Books
Limited
Text copyright © 2005 Rod Green

This edition published in 2005 by
Carlton Books Ltd
A Division of the Carlton Publishing Group
20 Mortimer Street
London
W1T 3JW

A CIP catalogue record for this book is
available from the British Library.

ISBN 1 84442 477 4

Executive Editor: Amie McKee
Art Director: Clare Baggaley
Design: Michelle Pickering
Production: Claire Hayward

Printed and bound in Singapore by Tien Wah P

THE CAT

Artlist Collection

CRAZY **CATS**

CARLTON
BOOKS

Persian

Persian

Persian

Persian

Scottish Fold

Mixed Breed

Mixed Breed

Oriental Shorthair

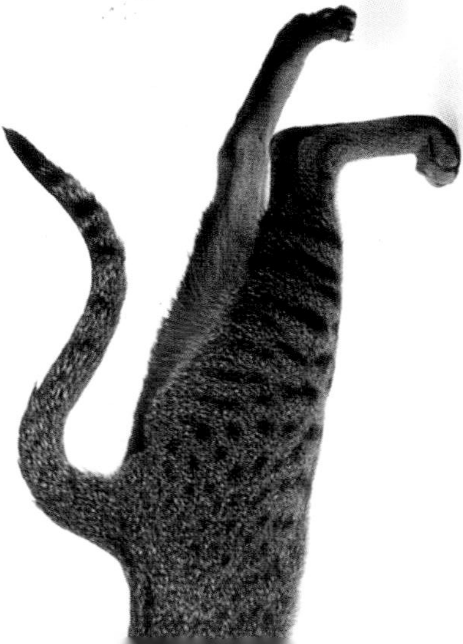

Oriental Shorthair

Oriental Shorthair

Norwegian Forest Cat

Mixed Breed

Mixed Breed

Burmese

Burmese

Burmese

Munchkin

American Curl

American Curl

Singapura

Singapura

Singapura

Singapura

Bengal

Bengal

Mixed Breed

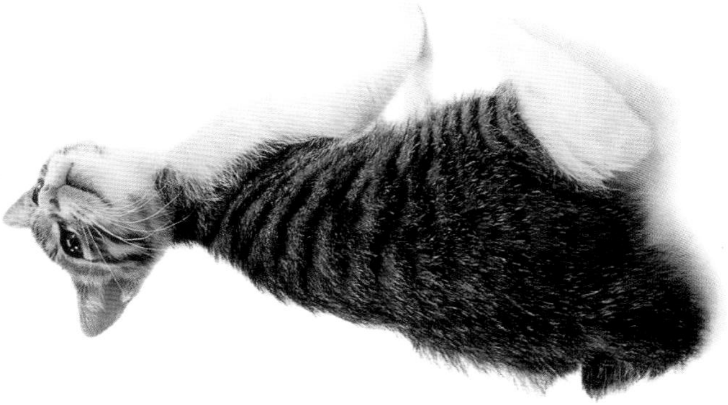

Ocicat

Ocicat

American Shorthair

American Shorthair

Somali

Somali

Somali

Mixed Breed

Russian Blue

Mixed Breed

Abyssinian

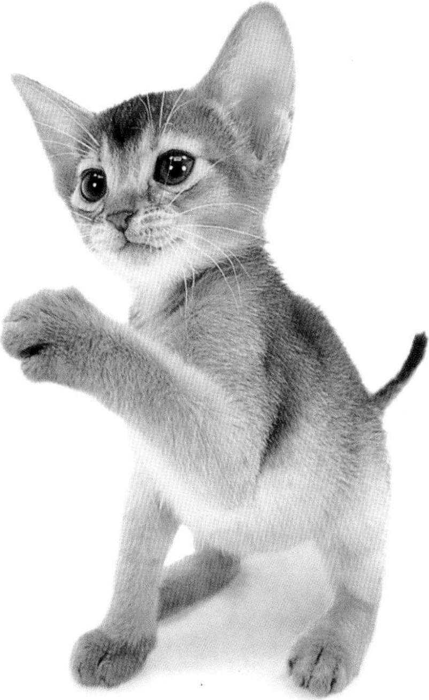

Abyssinian

Exotic Shorthair